Affirmations
for Life

Powerful Intention Statements for
Wellbeing, Positivity, and Happiness.

- Commanding Life -

Affirmation for Life. Powerful Intention Statements for Wellbeing, Positivity, and Happiness.

Copyright © 2021 by Commanding Life

Cover Image by Madison Taylor of TheHeroDraws.com

www.ShopCommandingLife.com

ISBN 978-1-7325400-8-8

Affirmations for Life

Affirmations are powerful, positive statements that can help direct your conscious and subconscious mind. Words can significantly influence your life and transform your internal state on a deep and profound level. When spoken with conviction, affirmations can improve your thoughts, emotions, beliefs, and behaviors. They work because they can program your mind into accessing and believing the repeated statements and concepts.

Intentionally using affirmations can create change toward the right inner environment to fuel the manifestation of your dreams. They will help you stay focused on how you want to feel. Motivate you to act and remain inspired by your goals. Change your negative thought patterns into positive ones. Influence your subconscious mind to access new beliefs. Help you feel positive about yourself and boost your self-confidence. Empower yourself, use the following affirmations to master your wellbeing, stay positive, and develop consistent happiness.

I am committed to my happiness, and I am making progress every day. I am finding peace with my pace as I transform into the person I know I am destined to be. I release where I have been. I accept where I am. I am excited and hopeful about where I am going. As I continue to commit to my joy, I trust the process taking me to what I desire. I am proud of who I am becoming.

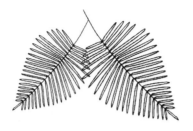

I trust that things are always working in my favor. I trust that I am showing up and making great choices. I trust that I will have what it takes to conquer what challenges me. I trust that I am doing what I should be doing to ensure my win. I trust that I have who I need with me supporting my moves. I trust that when I let go, I am making room for abundant goodness. I trust my ability to be happy.

I am confident in my ability to create the life I deserve. I believe that I am Divinely supported, and I am given the resources to thrive. I always have what I need, when I need it, and right on time. I am provided for, and this gives me the confidence for success. I am making my happiness a priority, and I am going for it all. I deserve the best life has to offer.

I am hopeful that everything is working out for me. The path to my success is open and clear for my journey. Supportive people and resources are aligning. Solutions are falling into place. I trust all is well. I have prepared, and I am ready to receive my miracles manifesting quickly. I am moving into a season of blessings. I am ready.

I am praising for my manifestation before I pray and ask. I am believing in myself before I back down. I am listening for guidance before I express my doubt. I am confidently stepping forward before I stand still in fear. I am trying before I quit on myself. I am doing all I can before I question my abilities. I am thanking before I receive my all. I trust that I am being blessed.

No matter where I am on my journey, I have decided to keep my thoughts positive and hopeful. Every step I take gets me closer to what I desire. I know energy goes where my attention goes. I am choosing to live my life concentrating on happiness, love, abundance, and success. I am focused on good things, and great things flow to me.

I am focused on what I want to manifest and how I want to feel. I am focused on appreciation for all the blessings in my life and my ability to create more. I am focused on my healing and moving forward with forgiveness. I am focused on my prosperity as I embrace the abundance flowing easily to me. I am focused on welcoming all that I need to thrive.

I am always growing and getting better. My past does not define me, and I am creating my possibilities in the now. I am compassionately allowing myself to change into the person I want to become. I am focusing on my happiness. I am pursuing the abundance I am worthy to receive. I am always transforming for the better. I am destined for greatness.

I am releasing my focus on the pace my dreams are manifesting. I trust that I can have the happiness I want, and I am confident in my ability to pursue it. Everything I am preparing for is coming effortlessly to me in perfect timing. I will focus on the good that is happening and use it to create more of what I desire. Abundant goodness is always flowing to me.

I am aligning with all that I desire. I
am aligning with the wholeness that
comes from healing. I am aligning
with the amazing version of myself I
have been working on. I am aligning
with the life of prosperity I have been
creating. I am aligning with the loving
relationships I am worthy of. I am
aligning with the peace that comes
from purpose. I am aligning with the
miracles manifesting for me.

I am creative enough to find solutions to move forward. I am in control of my happiness, and I am capable of steering my life in the direction I want. I am strong enough to conquer what challenges me. I am courageous enough to make changes to my mindset and live the life of abundance I desire. I have all that I need ALL ready within me.

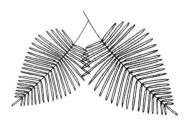

I am connecting with the fullness of who I am. I am proud of my transformation and my efforts to pursue what I deserve. In loving myself, I understand how to love and be loved. I recognize that self-first is not selfish, but a way to a better me. I am attracting people who love, support, and respect my uniqueness. I am amazing, and I know it.

I am learning to release with ease. I am gracefully letting go of all that's not serving the best version of who I want to be. I am moving on from old habits and the limiting thinking that's been holding me back. I am forging forward in faith and I trust in my ability to create the life I want. I am embracing and making room for the abundant miracles manifesting for me.

I am aligning with my fullness.
I am peace full.
I am plenty full.
I am success full.
I am joy full.
I am faith full.
I am beauty full.
I am great full.
I am hope full.
My life is full of abundant blessings.

I am in control of my life. I am
confident, and I believe in myself. I
am learning to embrace the wisdom I
developed from my past experiences
and use them for my benefit. I am
growing and going after the future I
want. I am pursuing my goals and
crushing them. Every day, life is
getting better and better for me.
Things are working out in my favor.

I am focused on a fruitful future. I am creative, and I find solutions with ease. I am abundant, and I am a magnet for more. I am making great choices and significant improvements. I am aligning with the best version of myself. I am making progress with my dreams. I am manifesting miracles with every moment I spend in gratitude. I am blessed, and I appreciate my life.

I am happily embracing the transformation I am experiencing. I am trusting the process because it is preparing me for the next chapter of my life. I am moving onto the new and believing that things are aligning in my favor. I am never losing; I am learning and leveling up. I know all is well, and big beautiful blessings will manifest at any moment.

I am blessed with a life full of love. I am surrounded by people that support and uplift me. I love being myself around them. I know that they are there for me, and I can rely on them when needed. They believe in me and my dreams. They want to see me win. I am grateful for the fantastic people in my life. My circle of love is a blessing.

I am excited about the blessings
pouring into my life. I am trusting that
I will be in the right place at the right
time to receive them all. I am faithful
that Source is supporting my journey.
I am grateful for the opportunities,
cleansing, healing, success, and
progress that I am experiencing. My
growth inspires me, and I welcome
more miracles manifesting.

I am a good person doing the best I can at any moment. I will be patient, kind, and compassionate with myself as I keep trying. I am learning and growing from my experiences. I will focus daily on loving who I am and caring for my wellbeing. My self-love is the feeling, and my self-care is a continued practice. I deserve the best life has to offer.

I am clear about what I want and what makes me happy. I know what I deserve, and I am going after it. I am worthy, and I am enough. I am at peace with where I am. I trust that I have what I need to succeed already within me. I can control the future I want, and it will be amazing. Big beautiful blessings are manifesting for me.

I am living up to the best expectations I have for myself. I have released all limits on my ability to triumph. I have emancipated myself from the thoughts of lack. I have embraced my potential to have everything I desire. I am committed to leveling up to more. I am dedicated to giving myself all. The track to success is clear for me. I will be victorious.

I am fearlessly stepping out of my comfort zones and improving who I am every day. I am excited about the progress I am making as new doors open for me. I am confident in who I am becoming and where I am going. I am joyously allowing more love and abundance into my life. Success is my destiny, and thriving is my birthright. Happiness is unfolding all around me.

I am excelling in everything that I do. Beneficial habits are becoming easy to practice consistently. I am attracting good results and positive outcomes. I am making great choices. I am responding to situations with confidence in my abilities. I am very capable of creating the life I want. What I desire is already on its way to me. Everything is always working out for me.

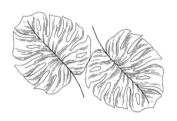

I am dedicated to attracting what I want. I am a magnet for prosperity because I believe in my ability to create all. I am a magnet for love because I work on the best version I can be. I am a magnet for peace because I am focused on my alignment with who I am. I am a magnet for joy because I am always grateful for my blessings. I am welcoming ALL that I need to thrive.

I am getting better at living in the moment. I am releasing my past because it cannot be changed. I am embracing the possibilities of my future. I am actively creating more love, peace, and abundance in the now. I am getting better and better every day at thriving. I am aligning with the fullness of who I am. I am blessed, and I am happy.

I am attracting unlimited abundance into my life. I am embracing my power of creation and transforming what I have into more. I am grateful for what I have, and I am excited about what is on the way to me. More love, peace, prosperity, and opportunities are aligning for me. I expect beautiful miracles spontaneously manifesting for me.

I am making the most of where I am.
I have learned from my missed takes,
and I am using new opportunities and
knowledge to create my reality. I have
many chances to make more of what I
desire in my life. I am releasing what
has gone, and I am excited about
what is to come. I know all is well.
Things will work out for me. I am
ready to receive what I have been
preparing for.

I am worthy of all that I desire. I love
who I am because I am an amazing
person that overcame challenges, and
I succeeded. I may have been tested,
but I definitely have triumphed. I am
patient as I prepare to welcome all
that is meant for me. I am deserving
of big beautiful blessings. I trust in
Divine timing.

I have an abundance mindset. I have
unlimited chances to create what I
want. I know that no matter what
leaves me, there is always more
coming toward me. I believe in more
love, more money, more friendships,
more opportunities, and more
possibilities. I deserve more, and
today I am welcoming more. More is
my mood and mindset.

I am silently winning battles and improving my life. I am proud of every step I am making because I am committed to forging forward. I am moving in the right direction. My choice to pursue my happiness makes me gratified. I am doing a great job with my healing and happiness. I am a victor.

I am proud of the progress I am making in my life. I am grateful for the transforming mindset that is helping me pursue the success I want. I am inspired by my growth and continued focus on creating more. I am moving past what has gone, appreciate what remains, and looking forward to what's to come. Things are working out for me. Life is good to me.

I am gently letting go and learning not to fear what the future holds. I am taking control of my life and embracing and enjoying my journey. I am slowing down and tuning in to my inner guidance. I am trusting myself and my ability to create what I want. I already have everything I need within me to succeed. I am ready to unleash the self-confidence that I possess.

I am never losing; I am always learning. I am compassionate and patient with my missed takes. I will keep trying. Every day I am more confident in my capacity to pursue what makes me whole. I am proud of who I am becoming. I am improving my response-ability with my choices. I trust I have what I need to thrive. I am a powerful creator.

I forgive myself as many times as needed to feel good about where I am. I am learning every day to accept who I am. I know I am a fantastic person worthy of what I work for. I am doing my best, and that is all that matters. All my effort on my well-being is making me become the best version of myself. I am deserving of happiness.

I have many reasons to stay happy and grateful. I have made great choices and created significant improvements. I am making progress in my life, and I am motivated. I have made good things happen, and I expect more to unfold. Life is blessing me in bountiful ways. Things are working out in my favor. I am hopeful for a fantastic future.

I am already loved. I am already blessed. I am already supported. I am already winning. I am already improving. I am already healed and whole. I am already seeing miracles. I am already abundant. I am already at peace. Everything I want is ALL ready within me. How amazing is that?

I am ALL ready.

I am ready for what I prayed for. I have healed, prepared, and made progress with believing in my full worth. I have overcome, and I am thriving. I am happy with what I have been blessed with, and I am excited for what is yet to come. I am worthy of all good things. Big beautiful blessings will spontaneously manifest for me.

I am making a change in what I pray for. I am not praying; I am thanking. I am thanking for relief from the burdens of the past. I am thanking for the strength to stay present. I am thanking for the focus to find solutions amid my challenges. I am thanking for the capability to move beyond what keeps me from pursuing my plenty. I am thanking for my abundant blessings because all is well. I am thank FULL.

My experiences are moving me to the next level, and I am trusting the process. I am patient with my progress because I know great things are unfolding for me. I am always moving in the right direction of happiness and success. I am committed to living a life aligned with what I deserve. I am worthy of all good things.

I am setting the right intentions,
staying positive, and I am committing
to my dreams. I am making great
decisions that allow my desires to
unfold with ease. I am clear about
what I want. I am focused on my
happiness because I deserve it. I am a
magnet for miracles manifesting
effortlessly.

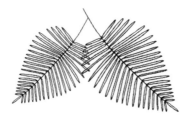

I am obsessively grateful for the loving
connections that surround me. I am
thankful for the supportive, devoted,
and kind people in my life. I am
appreciative of the opportunities I
have to create memories with them.
They bless me with their love and
respect. I am happy to be loved and
to give love.

Every experience I have is helping me grow. Everything is showing me who I am and who I need to be to have all the happiness I deserve. I trust that I am on the right path. What I go through is preparing me for success. I am worthy, and I know it. I trust I have what it takes to create what I want. I am leveling up, and I am ready for all good things.

I am making an effort to care for me more compassionately. My self-care choices are helping me understand how to love myself and share my love with others. I am lovable, and I am loving. I am attracting genuine love into my life. I am worthy of receiving the big beautiful love I give to others. I am ready to connect and create mutual partnerships.

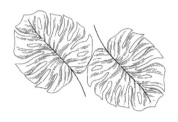

Everything I need is already within me. My experiences are helping me improve who I am. I am releasing what does not serve me, and I am developing a mindset that helps me thrive. Every day I am becoming more of who I want to be. I am practicing the right skills and talents to be successful. I am proud of my progress.

I believe that no matter what happens, I will be okay. I trust things are working out for me, and I am being guided to more of what I desire. I am confident in my ability to overcome anything just like I have in the past. I know that I am Divinely protected, supported, and provided for. I am blessed, and what I need is coming to me.

I am counting my blessings. I am
showing up for myself and trusting I
am Divinely supported. Doors are
opening for me, and things are
working out in my favor. What I want
is flowing to me with ease. I trust in
my journey, and I know I will get what
I desire. I am happy; today is going to
be a great day.

Today I am choosing to see greatness in everything and feel gratitude for all. I will honor the wholeness within myself with positive thoughts that encourage my thriving. I will focus on the good traits I possess. I will be understanding and compassionate with myself and my choices. I am doing a great job. I love me.

I am not complaining anymore; I am celebrating. I am not comparing myself; I am connecting with the greatness within me. I am not losing at anything; I am always learning. I am not letting go; I am leveling up to more. I am not giving up on my happiness; I am going after more.

I am choosing joy in my life. I am surrounding myself with people who motivate and inspire me. I am positioning myself for blessings and opportunities to win big. I am making what I want in life happen for me. I am patient because I know I am always making progress. I am very pleased with my efforts to build a better experience. My success is inevitable.

Today I am moving closer to where I want to be, and my dreams are coming true. I have committed to constructing what I desire, and everything I want is manifesting for me. I am flowing and aligning with the fullness of who I am, and I am creating a great life for myself. I am focused on my happiness, and I am doing a great job. I am proud of who I am becoming.

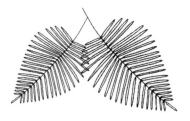

I am trusting that everything will be okay. I know that what is mine is on its way to me. Things are falling into place right on time. I am confident in my victory and my ability to create it. I know I am where I need to be, doing what I love, and creating my future. My life is working out for me. I am showing up for myself and my happiness.

I will connect with all that brings me joy. I will remind myself to be grateful and to acknowledge the abundant blessings that surround me. I will celebrate my victories as I continue to move forward. I will embrace the moments of love that flow easily to me. I will seek peace despite the doubt that can distract me. I will expect miracles to manifest effortlessly.

I know my thoughts reflect how I feel.
I am focused on having only positive
beliefs about myself. I am using my
words to be kind, uplifting, and
encouraging with everything that I do.
I will be compassionate, persistent,
and loving as I work on creating the
life I want. I trust that things will fall
into place and work out in my favor
right on time.

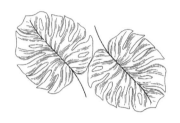

No matter what comes my way, I promise myself I will keep moving forward. I have made great progress and I am proud of my commitment to creating better. I owe it to myself to show up and continue pursuing all that I desire. I have decided what kind of life I want, and I am going after my happiness. I deserve success, joy, prosperity, love, and peace.

Life is too short to waste on negative thinking and habits that can hold me back. I am choosing to focus on the positive and the blessings in my life. I have everything I need, and I trust additional resources will show up. I am doing a great job with my wellbeing. I know that the more I am grateful, the more miracles manifest for me. I am blessed!

I believe in myself. I know I can win because I deserve happiness. I am strong, and I am enough. I know I have what it takes to be victorious and prosperous. I am going to make a beautiful life for myself. I will keep working on the mindset that helps me master the creation of the life I want. I am expecting to receive big, beautiful blessings.

I am manifesting beautiful things in my life. I am focused on self-love, self-compassion, and self-development. As I improve my belief about what I deserve, my outlook and positivity have expanded. I am the creator of my life, and I am focused on happiness and fulfillment. I value who I am, and I am doing a great job showing up for myself.

I am leaving what holds be back behind by forgiving and releasing my past. I am focusing forward on my fruitful future. I am directing my attention toward creating a better life for myself, and that makes me thrilled. I am doing a great job with the choices I am making and the progress I am creating. I am surrounding myself with love, peace, and prosperity. In everything I do, I find my joy.

I am focused on fine-tuning my senses. I clearly hear the comfort I need for my heart to be whole. I am seeing beyond my doubt and believe that better is on its way to me. I am touching others and blessing them with my kindness. I am tasting and enjoying the fruits of my labor as I become my happiest self. I am connecting with my peace, purpose, and prosperity.

I am always finding reasons to be happy with the life I have. I am doing a great job with my commitment to my wellbeing. Good things are unfolding for me because I am grateful for every blessing, big and small. The more I am thankful for in the now, the more I can attract for my future. I appreciate my life and what I am capable of creating. I am blessed.

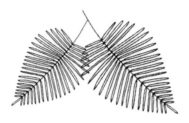

I am letting go of the doubts in my life, and I am holding on to my faith. My dedication to my happiness is why I will maintain my winning. I am making great decisions that are keeping me on the path to abundance and blessings. I am trusting that all is well, and things are working in my favor. What I want will manifest soon.

I am loving who I am becoming as I continue to challenge myself to be better every day. I am growing, evolving, and finding what makes me thrive. I am shedding what keeps me small, and I am building my big. I am transforming into who I am destined to be. I am clear with what I want, and I am going for ALL. I am blessed, and I know it.

I am trusting everything I desire is
already on its way to me. The
relationship I want is revealing itself.
The job I want is aligning with my
purpose and passion. The abundance
I want is pouring in through multiple
streams. The wellbeing I want is
becoming a natural way of life for me.
I am manifesting everything I want
with ease.

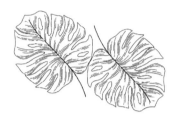

My heart is whole.

My body is healed.

My thoughts are positive.

My soul is inspired.

My future is bright.

My past is behind me.

My happiness is my choice.

My wellbeing is my priority.

My abundance is overflowing.

Life is working out for me.

I am focused on trust. Trust that
Source knows what I want and has
already prepared it for me. Trust that
I am being guided on my journey with
all the support that I need. Trust that
as I focus on gratitude, I am getting
closer to what I desire every day. I
trust that all is well, and blessings are
always flowing to me.

I am ready to release what does not serve my happiness. I am ready to receive abundance, love, and success in my life. I am ready to allow the Universe to guide me to my thriving. I am ready to be blessed with all that is meant for me. I am ready to live a life full of passion, purpose, and prosperity.

I am ALL ready.

I am loved, and I am loving. I am blessed, and I am a blessing. I am abundant, and I am abundance. I am supported, and I am supportive. I am peaceful, and I am in peace. I am creative, and I am a creator. I am joyous, and I am joyful. I am wholesome, and I am whole. I am healed, and I am healing. Balance is my true nature.

Everything I need is already within me. I am always receiving grace; life is good to me. As I surrender to the timing of my blessings, I know that I am Divinely guided to my abundance. I trust that I am doing enough to create the life I want. I am prepared to receive more than I can imagine. Everything I am working toward will manifest soon.

I am prepared for what I pray for. I have improved my behavior, thoughts, and habits for my good. I am consistent with my inner work and dedication to my happiness. My dreams are close to becoming a reality, and my breakthrough will be happening very soon. I am exactly where I need to be right now. I am doing a great job with my wellbeing.

I know that happiness starts with acceptance. I accept where I am and trust I will be provided with what I need to get where I want to go. Opportunities are lining up for me. I am not giving up on myself. I will rest if I need it, and then I will keep going. I will not quit on my happiness. I am worthy of having everything I desire.

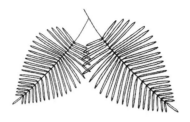

Clarity has replaced my confusion.

Faith has replaced my fear.

Focus has replaced my distraction.

Potential has replaced my pain.

Thriving has replaced my lack.

Wellbeing has replaced my worry.
Hope has replaced my helplessness.

Purpose has replaced my
procrastination.

All is well.

I am committed to my inner peace. I am focused on what balances my energy and what brings my soul joy. As I release the doubt that does not serve my growth, I welcome alignment with the faith I need to succeed. I will continue to work on my prosperity and trust I am Divinely supported. I am always guided toward the life I desire. The Universe has my back.

I am focused on being the best
version of myself. I am learning, and I
am leveling up. I know that I have to
be patient as I keep working on my
elevation. I am trusting in the Divine
timing of my life. Nothing can stop
my rise to the top. No one can pull
me back from the levels I overcame
and attained. I am proud of my
progress. I have all that I need to
keep thriving.

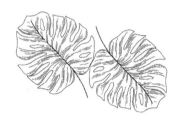

Endless opportunities to succeed surround me. Support is showing up and surprising me. Abundance is flowing freely to me. Miracles are manifesting for me. What is mine is already on its way to me. I am provided with what I need to get where I want to go. Life is good because I am focused on my happiness.

I release all the fears that limit what I think is achievable for my life. I release all the doubt in what I deserve. I release all the beliefs that hinder my worthiness. I release all the habits that hold me in the past. I embrace the possibilities for my future. I believe that big miracles can manifest quickly, and I am ready. I am faith FULL and open to the blessings that are possible.

I know that forgiveness comes in stages. I am patient with myself as I go back and forth between letting go and holding on. I am dedicated to my healing, and I am focused on my wholeness. I am confident that one day I will fully move on. I know that I may never forget, but I am willing to release the emotional hold the past can have. I am ready to be free to consistently focus on my happiness.

My choices reflect my focus and what I value. I value who I am and who I can be. I value the supportive, loving people that surround me. I value the growing peace that releases me from a past that challenged me. I value what makes my soul feel alive and inspires me to thrive. Most of all, I value my decision to focus on my happiness.

I understand that when the answer to my prayer is "yes," I am ready. I know that when the answer is "wait," I need to prepare for more. Source knows what I want and knows how to get me there. I know that when the time is right, what I desire will manifest. I release my impatience for results and trust every step of the way I will have what I need.

I welcome the ability to overcome the doubt that holds me back from going after more. I will never allow waiting to become a habit; I will enthusiastically live my dreams and take action. I will have fun and enjoy every day that I am given. I will push past my procrastination and embrace my ability to create abundance. I am in control of my happiness and success.

Every day I find something to feel
grateful for. When I appreciate what I
have, I find that I am blessed with
more. I have released my limiting
habits and thoughts, and I allow my
blessings to unfold in any form. I am
constantly surprised at how things
work out for me. I love how my
miracles are always manifesting.

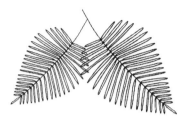

I am letting go of the resistance I have toward stepping into my full potential. I am embracing the vision I have for my life. I am rising to the level that I am being guided toward. I am receiving clarity about what I need to do and where I need to go. I am stepping into my greatness. I am confident because I am Divinely supported.

I am thankful for the blocks that kept me away from what I wanted; they redirected me to what I never knew I needed. I am grateful for the doors that closed; they lead the way to opportunities meant only for me. Life is always working out in my favor and providing me with what I truly desire. I am grateful for my blessings, no matter how they arrive.

I no longer allow my past to have
power over me. I have forgiven those
who have wronged me, and this
unburdened my soul. I have created
space within my heart to grow into the
loving person that I know I am. I feel
light, free, and ready to move forward
to write a new chapter. I have
discovered I am worthy of all good
things. I am encouraged to create the
life I want.

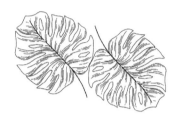

I am clear about what I want for my life. I am confident in what I can accomplish for myself. I am courageous in what I can achieve with my abilities. I am compassionate with myself as I try. I am kind to myself with the words I speak when I am alone. I am whole and complete because I already have what I need within me to thrive.

I am creating a new self-narrative, one
where I trust I already have what I
need within me. I am worthy of what
I am working on manifesting. I am
patient with myself as I pursue the life
I want. When I find myself falling
into old patterns, I will kindly
encourage myself to keep going
forward. The past has no power over
me. Right now, I choose to thrive.

I will work on improving how I speak to myself. I know my words have control in my life; I will use them to create more. I am building myself into who I want to be by ending the negative thought patterns that keep me from thriving. I deserve everything I work for. My words are impactful, encouraging, life-changing, and life-giving.

I can handle everything that comes my way with confidence. I can courageously overcome what challenges me with ease. Yes, sometimes, I have to rest and regain my strength, but I am always encouraging myself to keep winning. Nothing will stop my victory. I trust that I am Divinely supported, and the Universe has my back.

When I focus and set clear intentions, my faith keeps me believing that anything is possible for my life. I am always being blessed with opportunities. I am in love with the life I am creating for myself. Every morning I wake up with gratitude that things are working out for me. Faith and focus are my superpowers.

Anything is possible for me. My past showed me I am courageous enough to overcome anything that comes my way. My present reminds me I am always capable of improving and living life on my terms. My future inspires me to create more because I am worthy of unlimited possibilities. I am deserving of all, and I am going after it.

I am remaining positive about what is unfolding for me. I know that whatever happens is for my highest good. I have set my intentions, done my work, and prepared for what I want. I have released my limits, and I have leveled up to more. Things are falling into place right on time. Miracles are quickly manifesting, and I am happy.

I am attracting the resources that I
need right on time. Solutions are
showing up and resolving struggles.
Doors are opening, and new ways are
being made available. Bridges are
being built for better opportunities.
Paths are clearing and opening new
avenues. Everywhere I look, I find
support. I trust everything is working
out for me.

When I thought I could not survive, I made it through. When I believed I could not fall anymore, I started climbing. When I thought I was not going anywhere, I leveled up. I am proud of my progress and my willingness to do the work to create change. I am improving every day. I love and respect who I am becoming.

I am excited about the abundance coming my way. I am receptive to the solutions being presented. I am focused on what I want and where I want to go. I am making progress, and I am improving my mindset. I am working on my happiness, and I am actively building the life I desire. I trust that a way is always being made. I am expecting positive changes very soon.

Today I am embracing my ability to pursue the success and prosperity I desire. I am releasing the limiting beliefs that block me from seeing the possibilities manifesting in my life. I am worthy of all the great opportunities life is offering me. I am a powerful creator, and I am always blessed with what I need.

I am focused on the vision for my life.
I am passionate about my purpose,
and I am grateful for the skills that
allow me to succeed. I am seeing
significant progress manifesting. I am
inspired and motivated to keep going
after my dreams. I am effortlessly
creating abundance. What is meant
for me is naturally flowing in my
direction.

I am embracing everything unfolding in my life. I understand my full worth, and I am growing from my experiences. I know now that things are always working in my favor, even when I don't know why. I am trusting my decisions, and I will keep pushing forward. I am never failing; I am only learning. I am faith-full that I will always have what I need.

When I focus on my happiness, I am encouraged by how quickly new ideas flow to me. I am grateful for my growing ability to push past problems and focus on solutions. I already have everything I need to succeed within me. I believe in my talents, and I am happy with what I am accomplishing. I am proud of my growth.

I release my worry. I know that in the
near future, things will work out in my
favor. Solutions are already
manifesting because I have focused
my energy on happiness and
appreciation for my blessings. I trust
in my skills and ability to find a way
through. I will be victorious.

No matter what life sends my way, I am focused on the positive. I am gentle with myself as I learn how to level up. I am smart enough to succeed at what I try. I am stronger and more creative than I believe. I am more confident in my ability to complete what I started. I am blessed with considerable skills and resources to create success. I am always moving forward.

I am falling in love with who I am. I am giving myself everything by going after what I deserve. I believe in my infinite worth. I am focused on how I want to feel, and I am mastering my daily practice of self-care by being self-first. I am trusting that I have what I need to thrive. I am always Divinely provided for and supported. Life is good to me.

I am gentle with myself as I forgive past missed takes. I am grateful for what I have been through because I transformed into a better me. I realize that failures are a natural part of life; they help me evolve into who I am meant to be. My confidence is growing with every stage I conquer. My destiny is success and happiness.

I am focused on what I can control. I
am releasing what is not meant for me
to carry. I will keep improving my
mindset and elevating my beliefs. I
am making inspired choices with my
actions. Everything around me is
falling into place for my betterment. I
will remain optimistic as I pursue my
ALL.

At this moment, I accept who I am. I know I am worthy of the love, support, and abundance I am receiving. I am at peace with where I have been, and I am hopeful about where I am going. I am proud of my progress. Every day I work on my happiness. I am committed to my thriving.

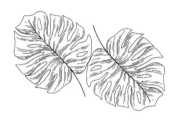

I am on a clear path to prosperity. I am taking control of my situation by making decisions that inspire positive change. I trust I am going in the right direction of what I desire. I am achieving what I want with ease. I am determined to develop the right environment that promotes my thriving. Success and happiness are mines to enjoy.

I have countless reasons to feel
blessed. Supportive people surround
me. Abundance flows freely to me.
Love is being drawn to me.
Opportunities for success are always
being presented to me. I am grateful
for the blessings I have. I love
everything about my life. I am a
magnet for miracles.

I release the negative thoughts and
beliefs that keep me stuck in the
patterns that hold me back. I am
choosing to focus forward and be
inspired by my progress. I am proud
of what I have accomplished and
where I am. I look forward to where
my improved mindset is taking me. I
believe in myself.

I am focused on the direction of my happiness. I am healing and embracing my full worth. I am releasing the resistance that blocks my creativity. I am allowing the transforming mindset needed to move from surviving to thriving. I am receiving Divinely guided inspiration that leads me to blessings in all forms. Miracles are manifesting for me. I am experiencing joy along my journey.

I am determined to succeed. I trust in my abilities to create the life I want. I am stronger because of my past. I am grateful for what I have in the present. I am more than enough, and I deserve a blessed future. I am confident that everything I need is within me and ready to emerge. I am a powerful creator.

I am deserving and worthy of happiness. Every day I tune into what brings me joy and fills my soul with peace. I am focused on my needs and how I feel. I am taking good care of myself. I am no longer standing in the way of my success. I am ready to receive the guidance that leads to my thriving.

I am always finding reasons to be grateful for what I have. In every moment, positive changes are unfolding for me. I am choosing to be happy now and not wait for things to be perfect. Abundant blessings are always present and available to me. I am surrounded by positive results that support my efforts to be happy. Life is good to me.

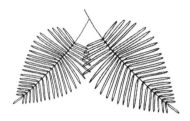

I am seeing opportunities manifest all around me. Obstacles have faded away. Concerns have been resolved. Doors have opened up to new possibilities. Bridges have been built to better. I am taking the time to celebrate my progress, blessings, and victories. I am excited about what is yet to come.

I feel safe and secure in my life. I know that whatever I choose to pursue will be successful. My ideas are supported, and I am supportive of others. Trustworthy people surround me. I have faith that my efforts will materialize, and my miracles will manifest. I am confident in my ability to create my desires.

Today I am determined to
concentrate on my happiness. I know
that wherever my focus goes will
manifest in my life. No matter what
unfolds, I am choosing to thrive on
the path toward my passion and
purpose. I will remain positive and
thankful for my blessings. Everything
is working out for me.

I am going with the flow. I recognize the power of grace when I get my yes. I appreciate the miracles that unfold when I receive my go. I understand the blessings behind a no. Life is working out for me better than I can imagine. I trust that everything is lining up perfectly for me in Divine timing. I am always given what I need right on time.

I know the best use of my imagination is creativity, not anxiety. I will overcome my doubts and do what needs to get done. I will master abundance by removing the limits of lack. I will strengthen my faith and overcome my fear. I will rise to the top and release what holds me back. I know I have what it takes to win.

I am learning my true worth and possibilities. I am thankful for the experiences that show me I am enough in every way. I do enough. I give enough. I am happy with my growing into my best version. Support shows up for me. Doors open up for me. Prosperity pours down on me. Every day I wake up grateful for what I have. I am effortlessly attracting more and more of what I want.

I am enough just the way I am. I am whole because I put effort into my healing. I am loved because I am loving. I am supported because I am supportive. I am abundant because I have released limited thinking. I love who I am and who I am becoming. I am destined for great things.

Every step I take develops my strength. Every limit I let go levels me up. Every good habit I develop unlocks my worth. Every choice I make empowers my confidence in my abilities. Every lesson I learn teaches me how to win even bigger. I am enjoying my journey of creating more.

I am positioning and preparing myself to receive the blessings I desire. I am aligning with abundance, and I am manifesting miracles with ease. I am making progress, and I am proud of who I am becoming. Every step I take gets me closer to my all. Everything is working out for me.

I am releasing my doubts about the levels I can attain. I am embracing the fullness of who I am. I know that I am worthy of great things. I am learning to trust myself and my abilities above all else. I am always in the right place at the right time, receiving abundant blessings.

I am welcoming what I need to thrive.
I am committing to positive habits
that serve my happiness. I am
embracing healing and the wholeness
of self-love. I am celebrating who I
am becoming. I am releasing the fear
that has held me back and moving
forward with faith. I am focusing on
the solutions that build my
abundance. I am expecting miracles
manifesting daily.

Obstacles will be removed.
Abundance will overflow.

Doors will be opened.

Connections will be made. Concerns
will be resolved.

Love will prevail.

Miracles will manifest.

Happiness will happen.

I am expecting a positive
transformation.

I am accepting all of who I am today.
I am releasing who I was yesterday. I
am hopeful about who I will be
tomorrow. I know that no matter what
happens, I am always moving
forward. Things are working out for
me because I am working on me. I
am proud of my progress.

I know that at this moment, I am
enough. Yes, I am working on
improving myself, but right now, I am
whole and complete. Happiness
begins with me. My journey is my
own to enjoy. I find something to
appreciate about myself every day. I
am worthy of all that I desire. I am
blessed; life is good to me.

I am enjoying my life. I am receiving spontaneous surprises and blessings that make me smile. I am always amazed at how good life is to me. I am finding reasons to be happy and being grateful for what I have. I am doing a great job where I am and where I am going. I love my dedication to creating the life I want.

I am a magnet for what I need in my life. The abundance I seek is showing up, and it is overflowing. The love I want is aligning with me, and I am prepared to receive it. The path I am on is clear and filled with opportunities. I know that I am being positioned to receive the blessings I desire. I am ready.

I am in the right place at the right
time. Every step I take prepares me to
succeed. Things are miraculously
working out for me. Blessings are
abundant, peace is prevalent, and I
am finding lots of joy on my journey.
I know that I am being guided to
more, and I am happy.

I am focused on my wellbeing. I will be self-compassionate as I keep working and releasing what holds me back. I will speak encouraging words to myself, and I will keep going after my dreams. I will celebrate my progress and welcome what brings my soul its peace. My happiness matters to me; I will do what it takes to feel good about me.

I am learning to have more faith in my inner guidance. I understand how to rely more on my intuition and ignore the past hurts that have misled me. I am retraining my brain to sustain a joyous lifestyle. I am forming new habits that are helping me focus on my happiness. I am trusting myself more, and it feels good. I am moving in the right direction of my desires.

I love the wholeness of who I am.
There are parts I am improving, and
parts I would not change. I know that
I was built from every brick thrown at
me, yet I am proudly and strongly
standing. No matter where I am on
my journey, I know that I am
deserving of everything I am going
for.

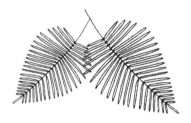

The better I become, the better I attract. My happiness starts with me and flows into my life and what I do. I am embracing my power of response-ability by choosing to work on who I am destined to be. I am aligning with my joy, and success is aligning with me. I will be happy and prosperous.

I am always growing, transforming, and moving forward. When I feel like nothing is progressing, I trust the silence does not mean failure. I will use the time to keep preparing for my victory. I know it is always still before dawn, and I have faith in my sunshine. I am ready to step forward and feel the warm sun on my face.

I am attracting more into my life.

My blessings are unfolding.

My abundance is building.

My love life is blossoming.

My path is opening.

My purpose is aligning.

My happiness is always happening.

I have what I want when I need it.

Life is good to me.

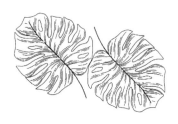

My patience is paying off. Everything I have been working on is falling into place. My blessings are manifesting, and the Universe is delivering right on time. I am exactly where I need to be, and things are working out for me. I am blessed, and I know it. I am happy.

I am focused on loving my life. I love how I am releasing my limits. I love opening myself up to the possibilities for my future. I love that I am Divinely directed, protected, and supported. I love how life works out for me. I am blessed and surrounded by great people. I am guided to my abundance. I always have what I need right on time. I am grateful for my life. Life is good to me.

I am grateful.

I am blessed, and I am a blessing.

I am love, and I am loved.

I am kind to myself and others.

I am guided to more.

I have everything I need.

I am celebrated.

I am progressing.

I am supported.

I am aligned with my highest good.

I love how I learn.

I love how I live.

I love how I level up.

I love how I thrive.

I love how I allow.

I love how I receive.

I love how I love.

I love how good things flow easily to me.

I love me.

I understand growth is never easy, but
I am trusting in my journey. I know
that I am always being guided to
more. I am learning lessons, and I am
not holding on to my mistakes. I
forgive myself for not knowing better
in the past. I celebrate myself for
working on being better for my future.
I've got this.

I am trusting that big blessings are unfolding in my life. I am on the right path, and I am moving closer to my manifestations. I am being provided with what I need right on time. I am joyously moving forward because I am making my good feelings a priority. I am creating the life I desire.

Today I am slowing down to witness the potential of my possibilities. I know that I am capable of creating my destiny. I am welcoming abundant opportunities opening up for me. I have what I need and what it takes to succeed. When I acknowledge the blessings in my life, I am welcoming more.

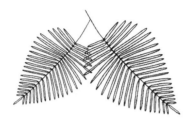

Every day I will create from a place of love. I will express gratitude for where I am. I will live with compassion. I will stand firm in what I believe in. I will not give up on my dreams. I will show up for my success. I will not back away from what I deserve. I will make my happiness matter.

I am receiving blessings, love, and Divine protection every day. I know that when I need support, all I have to do is ask for assistance. I can ask for wisdom to overcome doubt. I can ask for signs to encourage me to keep going. I can ask for grace to help me believe in my potential. I can pray for peace when the pain becomes overwhelming. Mostly, I can ask for renewed faith to keep trusting in my abundant future.

I am blessed. Things are working out in my favor today. The burdens of my past are washing away, and the optimism for my future is building. I am putting my energy and time into the activities and people I value. My efforts are paying off, and my abundance is growing. I have all that I need. Life is good.

What I have been praying for and working on is coming to me very soon. I have prepared, and I have been patient. While I have been waiting, I have been growing. My life is changing, and I am ready for success, love, and abundance to manifest for me. I am always moving forward.

I am excited about my future. I have done the work to remember my wholeness. I have focused on my positive feelings. I have prepared for my promise. The only thing left for me to do is welcome my win. I will be in the right place at the right time and marvel as my miracles manifest. Blessings are lining up for me.

I am trusting the process. I know that
what I want will happen. I believe that
the delay does not mean denied, and
more blessings are being made
available to me. I know that while I
prepare, I am doing enough, and I
am enough. I deserve all the good
things that are on the way to me.

Positive changes are happening for me. Everything I have been going through makes sense, and it is all coming together for my good. My worries are fading away, and my breakthrough is on its way. I will be in a different place that is full of blessings very soon.

I am at peace with who I am and where I am. Change has been challenging for me, but I am committed to my happiness. Where I am right now is where I am supposed to be. I am grateful for my blessings in the now. I will continue to create the future I want. I know that I am making progress, and I am always Divinely supported.

I am choosing to find the blessings showing up for me today. I am discovering what makes me happy to be alive, and I am using it to create more. I am optimistic about the good things that will manifest for me. Today will be a fantastic day. I am blessed; life is good to me.

I am thankful that I am not where I used to be. I have outgrown people and places, and I have leveled up. I am still learning and making progress. I have survived a lot, and I have become a better person. I am giving myself credit for all the work I am doing to be the best me. I am proud of the efforts I am making and the person I am becoming.

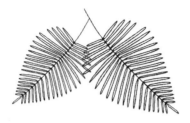

Great days are here, and more are lining up ahead of me. I am expecting favorable experiences very soon. I know that what is for me will arrive right when it should. I know that I don't have to force it or convince myself I deserve it. I release the worry, and I welcome the good. I am letting things flow to me. I am attracting everything I need. I trust in the timing of my life.

My past is behind me now. I have forgiven myself for anything that I have done that did not serve the highest vision for my life. I release myself from anything I am not meant to carry. I will live up to my fullest potential and align with the best within me. I am focused forward and I trust my ability to create what I want.

I am standing up for myself because I
am worthy of the happiness, love, and
success I pursue. I am confident in
my ability to set boundaries as I create
the life I want. I am true to myself,
and my authenticity shows. I am a
loving person, and good things flow
effortlessly to me. I accept who I am.
I love me.

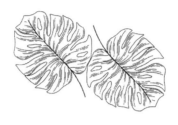

I am happy with my progress and my growth. Obstacles do not deter me; they only push me to go for my more. I am in-tuned with who I am, and I trust my ability to pursue my success. I am attracting the abundance, love, and support I am working on creating. I am committed to my happiness.

I am finding reasons to be at peace with my progress. I know that where I am is where I need to be. I am learning and growing at a pace that works for me. I am contented with where I am. Happiness starts with me and expands into all areas of my life. I will keep building my better.

I am consistently connecting with my good feelings. I am honoring my wellbeing when I work on my emotional wealth. I know that how I feel can determine where my focus goes. The better I am, the more I can create. I use gratitude to ground myself when I need to feel encouraged. I always have what I need. I am in a place of blessings.

No matter how exhausted I might get, I trust that better experiences are coming. I know that occasionally resting helps me regain my energy and the confidence to keep going. I am not quitting; I am recovering then getting back into the race. I am always the victor because I refuse to give up on myself.

I am taking the time to get to know who I truly am. I am releasing the feelings that weigh me down and embrace the ones that inspire me to thrive. I am learning to be comfortable with my past as I build my confidence for a beautiful future. I know that old chapters do not define me, but they empower me to create a new story. I am in control of my choices.

Today I invite peace into my life. Peace with where I am and where I have been. Peace with who I am while I work on transforming into a better version of me. Peace as I release the past and use my experiences to create the life I want. Peace as I maintain my patience and diligently prepare for my success. I am at peace as I persistently progress along my path.

Cheers to a job well done!

You have completed months of a fantastic journey. We hope the Commanding Life Affirmations for Life - Powerful Intention Statements for Wellbeing, Positivity, and Happiness helped you create more of what you desire. Great job on pushing forward, persevering, and making your happiness a priority. Today celebrate your victory and the incredible change you have created in your life from your routine of self-affirming actions. We invite you to check out more of our products, visit us at:

www.ShopCommandingLife.com

Made in the USA
Monee, IL
11 November 2020